# GET THE SCOOP ON Animal SNOT, SPIT & SLIME!

**Dawn Cusick**

## From Snake Venom to Fish Slime, 251 Cool Facts about Mucus, Saliva & More!

MoonDance

Quarto is the authority on a wide range of topics.
Quarto educates, entertains, and enriches the lives of our readers—
enthusiasts and lovers of hands-on living.
www.quartoknows.com

MoonDance

6 Orchard Road, Suite 100
Lake Forest, CA 92630
quartoknows.com
Visit our blogs @quartoknows.com

Printed in China
1 3 5 7 9 10 8 6 4 2

# CONTENTS

# INTRODUCTION

*WELCOME* to a world of snot, spit, and slime! You have probably noticed that many things in nature seem gross or confusing when you first learn about them. Why do some frogs spend dry seasons in mucous cocoons, for example? Or how is snake venom part of saliva? Without mucus and saliva, though, most animals would die. Here are just a few reasons why.

## EATING

*For vertebrate animals, mucus and saliva dissolve food and move it down to the stomach. Many invertebrates also use mucus to help them eat, making strings, nets, and blankets from mucus to help them catch food. Some animals add toxins to their mucus and saliva to catch prey. Other animals make mucus a part of their everyday diet. Yum.*

## BREATHING

*Mucus helps keep animal lungs clean. It also helps keep lungs moist, which makes oxygen and carbon dioxide move in and out faster. Animals without lungs still need to get oxygen into their bodies and carbon dioxide out. Keeping their skin moist with mucus does the job. Remember that the next time you hear someone talk about slimy earthworms and salamanders.*

### PROTECTING

*Many animals use chemicals in their mucus to protect them from predators, bacteria, and fungi. Other animals coat themselves in saliva or mucus to cool their bodies. Think about that the next time you're enjoying air conditioning on a hot summer day.*

### COMMUNICATING

*Animals use mucus and saliva to talk to each other with chemicals. Mammals use saliva to know which young are theirs, while predators track prey from chemicals in their slime trails. Some marine animals use chemicals in mucus to find other members of their species or avoid predators. Aren't you glad humans use words to communicate?*

### BUILDING

*Some animals use mucus and saliva like Super Glue to build homes and attach their bodies or eggs to surfaces. Imagine building a living room or a couch from mucus . . . how well do you think that would work out?*

*Have fun getting the Scoop on animal Snot, Spit & Slime!*

# MUCUS 101

*Mucus may make people say ewww, but most mucus is more than 95 percent water. Mucus may also have things in it that help animals defend themselves or talk to each other.*

## Chemistry Class

Mucus comes from a group of gooey proteins called mucins. Some mucins have sugars or lipids attached to them. Sometimes, sticky gels that animals release are called mucus, too.

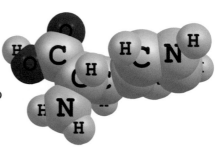

## The Slime Factor

Most mucus expands when it touches water. For animals that live in water, this slimy swelling makes mucus even more useful. Jellyfish bodies, for instance, are made from mucins and water.

## The More, the Merrier!

Humans have at least eight kinds of mucin genes. Some animals have more than eight.

## Where Does It Come from?

Mucus is made and released by mucous cells. Some people call them goblet cells because they look like the old-fashioned drinking glasses called goblets. Other people use the more formal name, collocyte. The word *collocyte* comes from the Latin word for glue, **collo,** and the Greek word for cell, **cyte.** In some animals, they are called mucocytes (**muc** for mucin and **cytes** for cells).

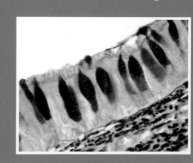

# MUCUS 101

## Snot Colors

Mucus comes in a rainbow of colors. Rats have red eye mucus when they are stressed or sick. Some sea snails have purple-blue mucus that people once used to make clothing dye, while clams make lots of Jello-like brown mucus to protect themselves from algae. Human mucus can be yellow or green when we're sick.

## Blood Mucus?

Hippopotamuses release reddish-brown mucus to keep their skin cool because they do not have sweat glands like most other mammals. Chemicals in the mucus work like sunscreen to protect hippos from the sun. Other chemicals in the mucus protect them from bacteria. Before people did experiments on hippopotamus mucus, they thought hippos looked red because they were bleeding!

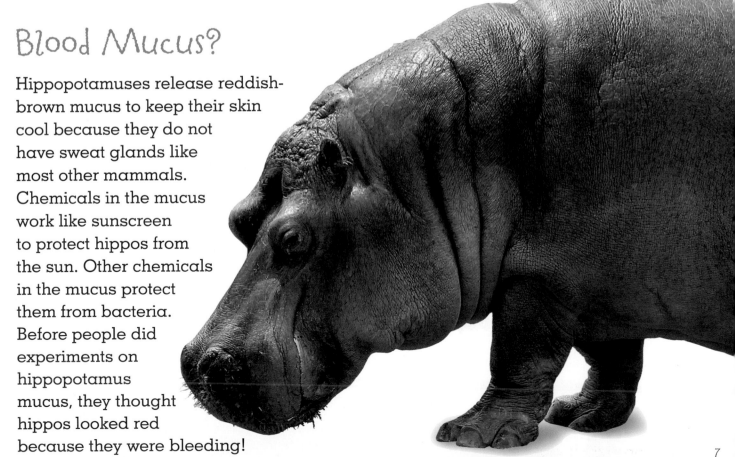

# MUCUS 101

*Mucus protects animals in many ways. Some mucus protects animals from infections caused by bacteria or fungi. Other mucus cleans and protects animals from dirt, acids, and chemicals.*

## Check It out

From horses to humans, mucus lines the long tube that starts with the mouth and ends with the anus. Mucus protects the esophagus from sharp foods. Mucus protects the stomach and small intestine from acid. Mucus helps small food molecules move into the bloodstream. It also protects the large intestine from feces. Wow!

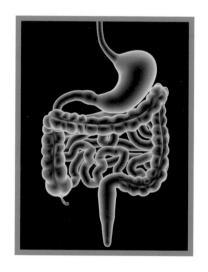

## Gross?

People make about four cups of mucus a day. When we're sick, we make extra mucus that is often thicker. Where does all this mucus go? Usually, we swallow it.

## Extra Mucus

Carnivores and carrion eaters have stronger stomach acids. Extra stomach mucus protects them from these strong acids.

## Extra-Thick Mucus

River otters use an extra-thick mucous layer to protect their esophagus from sharp spines on the fish they eat.

# MUCUS 101

## Take a Deep Breath

Mucus lines the insides of the branching tubes in vertebrate lungs, working to remove dirt, chemicals, and other small particles. When mucus catches things that don't belong in our lungs, we can cough it up from our lungs and out our mouth. Mucus lines our bladders, too.

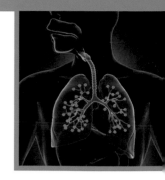

## Mucous Machines

The mucus that lines our nasal cavities is made in our sinuses, which are lined with goblet cells. Other vertebrate animals have sinuses, too. Imagine how much mucus an elephant's sinuses need to make to line the inside of its trunk!

## The Nose Knows

When something's in your nose or the back of your throat that does not belong there, you get the urge to sneeze. Small drops of mucus leave the nose with great force, traveling far and fast.

## Can You Hear Me Now?

Did your voice sound funny the last time you had a bad head cold? If too much nasal mucus blocks your sinuses, your voice can sound muffled.

# MUCUS 101

*Mucus helps all animals by moving important gases and chemicals into and over their bodies. This kind of movement is called diffusion. In case you are wondering, the word diffusion rhymes with the word confusion.*

## Dr. Mucus to the Rescue

In many animals, mucus has chemicals in it that kill bacteria and viruses. Fish, frogs, earthworms, and corals are just a few of the animals that have these chemicals in their mucus.

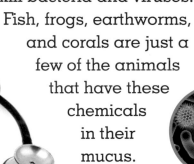

## Moist Mucus

The water in mucus helps keep lungs moist. Nose and throat mucus also helps keep the air we breathe in moist. Oxygen and carbon dioxide gases diffuse faster across moist lungs and skin.

## Diffusion Confusion?

Still confused? Let a pair of stinky socks clear things up. Imagine your best friend washes his or her socks only once a year. Boy, do those socks ever stink. If your friend takes off his or her shoes in the far corner of your room, it won't be long before you smell those stinky feet. Why? Because those stinky sock scent molecules will move all by themselves from the place where there are many of them (the socks!) to the places where there are fewer of them. Diffusion happens all by itself.

Don't believe it? Add a few drops of food coloring to a glass of water. Watch the dye diffuse through the water. Having fun? Do it again with hot water.

## Poisonous Mucus

Poison dart frogs (right), warty newts (below), and some other amphibians use their mucus to spread out toxins. Some frogs have chemicals in their skin mucus that keep mosquitoes away, too.

## Eye Boogers?

Whether you call them eye boogers, sleepy seeds, or eye crust, the crunchy grit in the corners of your eyes when you first wake up in the morning is very normal. Eye crust is made of hardened mucus, oil, and dead cells.

## Blinking Mucus

Blinking our eyelids moves mucus, oils, and dirt away before they harden. Think about that the next time you're part of a staring contest!

## No Tears Here

Seals, sea lions, and walruses have extra mucus on their eyes that protects them underwater. When the mucus dries around the outsides of their eyes, it can make them look like they have been crying.

# BREATHING SLIME

*Although they do it in different ways, all animals need to move oxygen into their bodies to help their cells make energy. Animals also need to move carbon dioxide out of their bodies. Mucus helps gases move faster.*

## Small Lungs

Compared to other vertebrate animals, most amphibians have very small lungs. They need more oxygen than these small lungs can handle and skin mucus helps them get it.

## Named After Slime

Instead of small lungs, slimy salamanders have no lungs. They use a thick layer of sticky mucus to help their skin stay moist and to get enough oxygen.

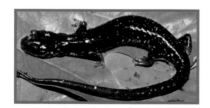

## No Lungs

Earthworms, nematodes, and many other invertebrates use their skin as breathing organs. Mucus makes oxygen and carbon dioxide move across their skin faster.

## Breathing Eyes?

Mucus is part of the film that covers the eyes of many animals. It also helps oxygen and carbon dioxide diffuse across the eye. This movement is important because eyes do not have as many blood vessels as most other parts of the body. The film also helps us see better and protects the eyes from dirt.

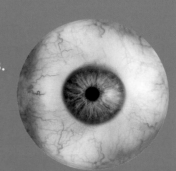

# BREATHING SLIME

## Snot Spouts

When whales surface, they exhale a mix of gases, water, and mucus through their blowholes. Some marine biologists use small drones to collect spout mucus for research.

## Eel Skin

Even though they are fish and have gills, eels get more than half of their oxygen through their mucus-covered skin.

# NOSE MUCUS

*Nose mucus does important work: it stops dirt and pollen from getting into an animal's lungs. It also helps animals smell, which helps them find food and avoid predators. Let's hear it for nose mucus!*

## Clean-up Crew

In mammals, mucus catches dirt and germs in nostrils. Next, small hairs called cilia sweep the dirt and germs to the back of the throat and down to the stomach.

## Booger Recipe

Mix together mucus, dirt, and other debris in an animal's nostrils. Allow the mucus to air dry as the animal breathes. What do you have? A booger!

## Smell This!

Nose mucus also helps animals smell. Scent molecules dissolve in wet mucus. Nerve cells collect the scent information in the mucus and send it to the brain.

## Shock Your Science Teacher

Instead of the word *booger*, try using the scientific term: nasal detritus. *Nasal* means nose, and *detritus* means waste or trash.

# NOSE MUCUS

## Nose Pickers

People may be grossed out to see primates picking their noses. Removing hardened mucus from their noses helps keep their nostrils moist, which helps them smell nearby predators and foods.

## Yum, Yum?

Why do gorillas, chimpanzees, and some other primates eat their boogers? In the wild, there is so much competition for food that even low-energy boogers are worth eating.

## Spicy Snot

Spicy foods can cause extra mucus to come running from your nose.

## Frozen Snot

Many animals make extra mucus in cold weather. Nasal mucus can freeze when it's cold enough.

*Many animals use sticky mucus to help them find food and survive in the wild.*

## Sucker Mucus

Leech suckers release acidic mucus that helps them cling to the animals they feed on. Mucus in their saliva also helps dilute the blood they feed on.

## Happy Hunting

How do you catch food if you're a carnivore without paws or fangs? With a sticky tongue, of course! Frogs, toads, and chameleons use a gland in their mouths to make the glue-like mucus that coats their tongues.

## Toe Snot

Tree frogs use a combination of sticky mucus and flat toe tips to climb trees.

**Chameleon catching fly**

# STICKY MUCUS

## Tadpoles on Board!

Unlike most other frogs, poison dart frogs release their eggs in trees instead of water. The tadpoles still need water, though, so father frogs carry the tadpoles to nearby water on their backs. Sometimes, females help move the tadpoles. Sticky mucus prevents the tadpoles from falling off.

# TRAVELING MUCUS

*For most animals, moving quickly from one place to another can help them find good food and homes, or escape predators. Moving fast takes a lot of energy. Mucus helps!*

## Gliding Slime

Snails and slugs use their strong, muscular foot to travel over rough ground and up and down trees and other surfaces. Their mucus helps them move in two ways. First, its glue-like stickiness helps them hang onto the surface they are traveling on, even if they're upside down. Second, when their foot muscles push against the mucus, the mucus becomes more like a liquid, helping them glide.

## Soil Slime

Mucus helps earthworms move through soil and burrows. Just one backyard can have thousands of earthworms in it. That's a lot of mucus!

## Double Trouble

Some animals have glands that can very quickly release mucus and other glands that can very quickly help dissolve mucus. The animals can use these duo-glands to help them move. Stick/unstick, stick/unstick, stick/unstick . . . over and over again. Sea stars, sea urchins, planarians, and some other animals move this way.

# TRAVELING MUCUS

## Slimy Speed

Fast-swimming fish such as barracudas use a mucous slime layer on their scales to help them move through the water with less drag. Even though it takes energy for their bodies to make the mucus, they end up saving energy because it's less work to swim with slimy scales.

# FISH SLIME

*Scales are part of a fish's skin, and are made from keratin, the same protein that makes up your skin. Fish use glands on their skin to make mucus. Fish that need a lot of mucus have extra or larger mucous glands.*

## Scale Size

Not all fish scales are alike. Fish with no scales or small scales tend to have more mucus. The extra mucus helps protect them.

The fish shown here are goby fish. They do not have scales so they have a lot of mucus.

## Toxic Mucus

Predators that eat goby fish often spit them back out because of the goby's toxic mucus. When biologists spread goby mucus over other types of fish, their predators refused to eat those fish, too.

# FISH SLIME

## Osmosis Mucus
## (Or, Why Do Freshwater Fish Pee So Much?)

When the inside of a fish's body is saltier than the water it lives in, water molecules move into the fish's body through its cells. If the fish did not get rid of this extra water, it would die. Freshwater fish often use a thick layer of mucus to stop some of the water from moving into their bodies. Water movement through cells is a type of diffusion called osmosis.

## Treat 'Em Right

Most fish release lots of extra mucus when people handle them. If you need to touch a pet fish, do it with a towel instead of your hands. Fish also release extra mucus when they are stressed by predators or their environments.

## Migrating Mucus

Fish biologists have been curious about how Atlantic salmon can migrate from fresh water to salt water for a long time. (Most animals cannot change the type of water they live in because of osmosis problems.)

## Slimy Experiments

When biologists tested the mucus in migrating salmon, they found these fish had more protein and antibodies in their mucus. The salmon may be making more antibodies to help protect themselves from sea lice and other marine parasites that they do not have in their freshwater habitat. They may also be trying to help their bodies deal with different osmosis problems because ocean water is saltier than their bodies.

# TALKING MUCUS

*Many animals use chemicals called pheromones (FAIR monz) to send and receive information. Mucus helps diffuse these pheromones over their bodies so the information can be shared.*

## Lying Mucus

Some filefish may use their mucus to hide from predators. Their mucus smells like the coral they live on, tricking predators.

## Nice to Meet You

Eels use skin mucus to find out the age and gender of other eels.

## Alarm Mucus

Many fish release alarm mucus when their skin is cut. Predators use alarm mucus to find injured prey, which may be easier to catch.

## Calling All Minnows!

Many schooling fish use mucous smells to help them come together in groups.

# TALKING MUCUS

## Sticky Situation

Ever wonder why the suckers on octopus tentacles work so well on predators and prey but never stick to their own suckers? The tentacles and suckers are covered with mucus, which helps nerve cells tell muscle cells when they should not contract.

## Snail Trails

Many land snails follow the mucous trails of other snails. Some snails use these trails to find prey or mates. Other snails snack on the debris left in mucous trails. When snails follow new snail trails, they do not need to use as much mucus when they move, which helps them save energy.

## Yuck, Fear Tastes Bad!

Some earthworms use mucus to mark their burrow trails. They also release alarm mucus when predators are close. Biologists have seen predators such as salamanders spit out earthworms when they are releasing alarm mucus.

## Better than GPS

Some slugs use their mucous trails to find their way back home. Sounds pretty cool, right? Unfortunately, snakes and other predators can use these trails to find dinner.

# HIDING MUCUS

Animals hide for many reasons. Some animals hide to avoid predators. Others hide from prey until right before striking.

## Sticky Mucus

Stubby squid bury themselves in sand during the day to avoid their predators. Sand sticks to their body mucus, hiding them well.

## Sand Camouflage

Instead of hiding in caves or between rocks, some eels hide under sand that sticks to their skin mucus.

## More Ewww

Young cereal leaf beetles hide from predators under layers of mucus and feces (poop). The mucous layers also help their bodies stay cool while they feed.

# HIDING MUCUS

## Sweet Dreams

Most types of parrotfish burp out lots of mucus before they sleep and spend the night under these mucous blankets. Biologists believe the mucus may protect the fish from eels. In lab experiments, eels ate parrotfish species that did not make mucous blankets, but did not eat the blanket-making parrotfish. After the eels tasted the blanket mucus, they left the parrotfish alone. Some wrasse fish sleep under mucous blankets, too.

# BUILDING MUCUS

*Mucus helps animals build homes for protection from predators and the environment. The glue-like strength of some mucus also lets some animals build lifetime homes in reef ecosystems.*

## Mucous Burrows

Some mantis shrimp and jawfish spend a lot of time hiding from predators in burrows. Mucus holds their sandy homes together.

**ABOVE:** Jawfish
**RIGHT:** Mantis shrimp

## Mucous Cooling

Water-holding frogs from Australia store water in their bladders and in pockets under their skin. The frogs spend the dry season buried underground in mucous cocoons made from many layers of shed mucus and skin. If they run out of their stored water, the frogs can eat parts of their cocoon to get moisture.

The Aborigines used to dig up water-holding frogs and gently squeeze them when they needed fresh drinking water.

# BUILDING MUCUS

## Upside Down

Young tunicates use mucous glue from their heads to attach themselves upside down to their adult home. The tunicates in the photo on the right are blue, and are living near sponges and corals.

## Building Reefs

More than 25 percent of the world's fish species live in coral reef habitats. Without mucus, there would be no coral reefs.

Young corals and sponges swim down to the ocean floor. When they find a good place to live, they attach themselves to their new home with super-strong mucus.

# DINNER MUCUS

*Mucus makes a fine meal for some animals, especially those that live underwater. Even though mucus does not have a lot of energy in it, there aren't many animals competing for it.*

## Mucous Armor

If a parasite gets too close to a fish's skin, the fish makes extra mucus and the parasite falls off.

## Mucous Signals

How do the fish being cleaned at cleaning stations know when a cleaner is eating their mucus instead of parasites or dead skin cells? Changes in their mucous layers tell them.

This triggerfish is not dead or sleeping. It's being cleaned by cleaner wrasse.

## Ouch!

If a cleaner fish bites into an electric eel's body mucus, the eel gives the cleaner an electric shock!

# DINNER MUCUS

## Thanks for Dinner

One type of South American catfish eats almost nothing except mucus from other fish. In one study, biologists found that 94 percent of the catfish's diet was mucus. The other 6 percent? Mostly algae.

## First Food

Who says only mammals make food with their bodies to feed their young? Some discus fish and Asian catfish feed their fry with extra mucus they release through their scales. Both male and female parents feed body mucus to their fry, and they do it for a few weeks.

## Dinner Slime

Some fungus beetles eat snail slime mucus. They also eat the fungi they live with. Think about snacking on snail slime the next time someone tells you to finish your vegetables.

# DINNER MUCUS

**Crab on coral**

**Larval crab riding a jellyfish**

## Poop Cleaners

For animals such as sponges and corals that do not have complete digestive systems, mucus helps remove body waste. Many types of crabs, lobsters, and shrimp feed on coral mucous waste. Some sponges give their feces-filled mucus to nearby corals. Other animals and bacteria also eat this poopy mucus.

## Beat It, Buddy

When jellyfish want to get rid of hitchhiking shrimp, lobsters, and crabs, they make extra mucus. Instead of leaving, the young lobsters and crabs eat the mucus!

Some crabs and shrimp want more than mucous waste from corals. To get fresh mucus, they make cuts in the corals. When the corals make extra mucus to protect themselves, the crabs eat it.

## Zombie Ants

Snails try to get rid of fluke parasites in their lungs by making mucous balls called cysts. The mucous balls leave the snails' bodies in their slime trails. When ants find mucous balls, they eat them. The parasites in the mucous cysts make the ants behave like zombies.

# HUNTING MUCUS

For many invertebrates, mucus makes a useful tool to catch food as it passes by. Sometimes the mucus covers the animal's body. Other times, mucus is released as strings, nets, and blankets.

## Mucous Filters

Animals called larvaceans live in ocean waters. To catch food, they build houses made from two mucous nets that work like filters. Larvaceans are a type of tunicate. Each animal is about two inches wide, but their mucous house can be six feet wide!

**LARVACEAN**

## Mucous Sinkers

Larvaceans let go of their mucous homes when the filters get clogged. The old mucous homes look like parachutes, and are called sinkers because they sink to the bottom of the ocean floor. When scientists at the Monterey Bay Aquarium Research Institute did tests on the sinkers, they found out many deep-water animals use sinkers for food. Some larvaceans make new mucous houses twenty times a day!

**Larvacean home**

# HUNTING MUCUS

## Mucous Nets & Strings

Many marine animals use mucus to help them filter feed on marine snow and plankton. Some marine snails and worms (right) catch prey in mucous nets. Many mussels (below left) and clams (below right) use mucous strings to capture food.

ABOVE: Windmill bamboo worms build tubes with spokes to live in. The worms fill the space between the spokes with mucus, which catches small pieces of food. To feed, the animals come out of their tubes and eat the food-filled mucus.

## Filter Feeding

Corals (left) and sponges use one kind of mucus to catch food and another kind to remove waste. Their mucus changes as they get older or when they live in deeper water.

## Mucous Show

Young glow worms in New Zealand spin silk tunnels and add drops of mucus to them. At night, small insects are attracted to the glow worms' light and get stuck in the toxic mucus. Tourists travel from all over the world to see the show.

# HUNTING MUCUS

## Hands-Free Feeding

Comb jellies (right) use mucous threads filled with stinging cells to hunt. The mucous threads stay coiled up until it is time to hunt, then the jellies use them the way cowboys and cowgirls use ropes to lasso calves.

## Stinging Mucus

Jellyfish keep layers of mucus over their stinging cells. Mucus holds the stung prey in place until the jellies can move it to their mouths. Some jellies carry around large sheets of mucus. Lion's mane jellies (above) are called snotties because they have so much mucus.

## Mucous Bells

Moon jellies catch food without stinging cells. The undersides of their bells are covered with mucus. When food sticks to the mucus, the jellies use their oral arms to move the food-filled mucus into their mouths.

## Mucous Light

Bobtail squids use mucus around their light organs to catch glow-in-the-dark bacteria. When they go hunting at night, the glowing bacteria help them blend in with moonlight.

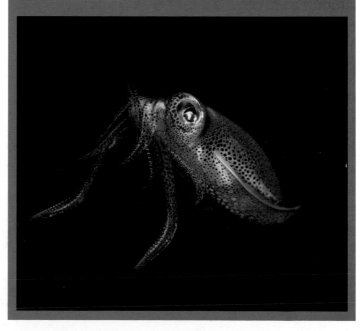

# DEFENSE MUCUS

*Animals use mucus to protect themselves in many ways. Sometimes, they release lots of mucus to make predators go away. Other times, their extra mucus works as a layer of protection.*

## You've Been Slimed!

Slime stars have thick skin and thick legs, which means they cannot escape from predators as quickly as other sea stars. When disturbed by a predator, they release a thick layer of toxic, bad-tasting slime.

## Thank You!

Marine flatworms called nudibranchs make mucus that protects them from coral, anemone, and jellyfish stings. When they eat these animals, their bodies keep the stinging cells for their own defense.

## You Can't Sting Me!

Many types of crabs and lobsters use mucus to protect themselves from coral, anemone, and jellyfish stings.

## Clownfish Habitats

Clownfish make special scale mucus that protects them from stinging cells in the anemone's mucus. This mucus lets clownfish use anemones as a habitat. Young clownfish start to make this mucus the first time an anemone stings them.

# DEFENSE MUCUS

## Cool Trick

How do you eat the most venomous insects on the planet? If you're a Texas horned lizard eating harvester ants, you do it by wrapping mucus threads around the ants before swallowing them. Yum!

## Lots of Mucous Glands

What's worse than lots of hagfish slime? Lots of hagfish slime mixed with protein threads that make the slime into a thick, gooey fabric! How can hagfish make so much slime? They have more than one hundred pea-shaped mucous glands so they can make a lot of slime very quickly. Even sharks and other large fish leave hagfish alone after they've been slimed.

## Slug Slime

Many slugs produce extra mucus when threatened. This thick slime layer makes them hard for predators to pick up. If a predator bites into them, slug slime can be so thick that predators spit the slugs back out.

# DEFENSE MUCUS

## Mucous Attacks

Many sponges and corals release lots of mucus when predators try to feed on them. Some predators give up when they get a face full of mucus. Others, such as the marine turtle below, eat the defense mucus. It does not have as much energy as corals and sponges do, but it's better than nothing.

# DEFENSE MUCUS

## Spiny Mucus

Stingrays store their venom in a sac filled with mucus. When stingray spines break into the flesh of another animal, the spines also break open the venom sac.

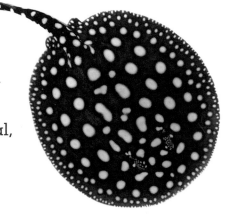

## Mucous Ink

Many octopuses, squid, and cuttlefish spray ink clouds when they feel threatened. Sometimes they hide in the ink; other times they use the cloud to confuse predators while they escape. The ink clouds come from a dark pigment mixed with a lot of mucus. Even newly hatched animals can release ink.

# TOXIC MUCUS

*Mucus does a great job of spreading the toxins that make animals poisonous or venomous. Many animals rely on these toxins for defense or to help them catch prey.*

## Toxin Thief!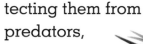

Pufferfish release strong toxins in their mucus. The toxins do not bother the copepod parasites that feed on pufferfish mucus. These toxins stay in the copepods' bodies, protecting them from predators, too.

## Toxic Spines

Lionfish have toxin-filled mucus on their spines. Even dead lionfish still have toxic mucus. How do people know that? When chefs try to make lionfish dinners at fancy restaurants, they have to wear special gloves. The heat from cooking destroys the toxins so it's safe to eat them.

## Invasive Toxins

Boxfish have mucous toxins, too. Like many other animals, their mucous toxins can spread into the water around them, which can be a problem when boxfish and other toxic fish move into new places.

# TOXIC MUCUS

## Toxic Defense

Cannonball jellies release toxic mucus when predators get too close. The toxins are not strong enough to kill a human, but they can kill small fish.

## Let's Dance!

Disco clams find food by using blinking lights to attract small animals. If a larger animal is attracted to the light or tries to attack, the clams release toxic mucus.

## Too Much of a Good Thing

In healthy fish, mucus helps to keep gills clean. When fish are exposed to the toxins in red tide, they die because their gills make too much mucus.

## Record-Setting Mucus

Box jelly venom can kill a human in minutes. Biologists from Australia have started "milking" box jellies to collect venom for drug research and anti-venom medicines. It takes a lot of work to remove toxins from the mucus around box jelly tentacles.

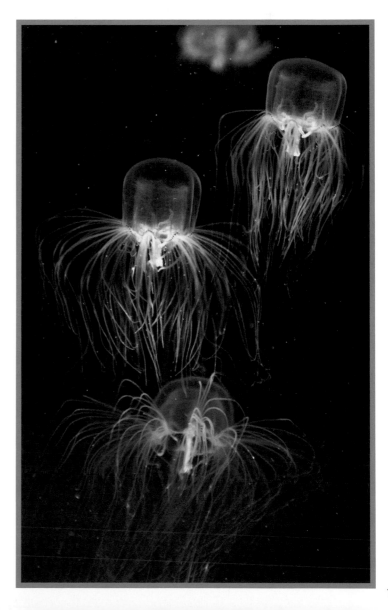

# GLUE MUCUS

*The glue-like nature of some mucus lets animals attach eggs to surfaces. This mucous glue is so strong that even heavy rains and strong ocean currents and winds do not break their bonds.*

## Crustacean Nation

Many crustaceans glue their eggs to their bodies as a way to protect them. In some species, only males glue the eggs to their bodies. In other species, females do it, too. At right, look for a crab's eggs on its abdomen. Below, check out the pink eggs covering a peacock mantid shrimp's abdomen.

## Sleeping Glue

Snails use mucous glue to attach their eggs to a surface and to keep them together. When female apple snails glue their eggs in place, they often add extra mucus. The extra mucus slows down the amount of oxygen that moves through the eggs to the embryos inside. With less oxygen, the embryos grow more slowly so the eggs do not hatch until after the dry season passes.

# GLUE MUCUS

## Snail Glue

Marine flatworms called nudibranchs (above and right) glue their brightly colored eggs in groups shaped like ribbons. In the photo at the right, the nudibranch eggs are yellow. In the photo to the far right, the eggs are orange.

## Mucus & Sand Camo

Another marine snail, the moon snail, uses extra mucus to glue its eggs together. Sand sticks to the mucus and helps the egg mass camouflage with the ocean floor.

## The Right Place at the Right Time

Many female insects glue their eggs to the plants their young will eat after they hatch. Above, a ladybug is laying and gluing her yellow eggs to the underside of a leaf. At right, green butterfly eggs have been glued to a leaf.

# WILD & WACKY

## Polluted Mucus

Earthworm mucus can absorb toxic metals from polluted soils. These metals would kill the earthworms if they entered the worms' bodies. Instead, the metals stay in the mucus.

## Mucous Pollution

The surfaces of some oceans are covered with a mucous layer called sea snot. Scientists are not sure why sea snot blooms come and go. They may be tied to the stresses some ocean animals go through when waters become warmer or more acidic.

## Shark Snot

Some sharks use a snot-like gel on their heads to bring electrical signals from bleeding prey to their brains.

## Floating Glue

Many newly hatched fish and tad-poles use sticky glue from their heads to help them stay near the water's surface while they feed.

## No Milkshakes?

In some people, dairy foods cause a reflex that makes extra mucus. Singers and public speakers often avoid these foods before performing so they won't have extra mucus on their vocal cords.

## Mucous Tubes

Female giant squid lay their eggs in mucus sacs that look like large tubes. SCUBA divers recently found a giant squid's mucous tube that was more than twelve feet wide!

# WILD & WACKY

## Mucous Bubbles

Some fish place their eggs in mucous bubbles that float on the water's surface. The sticky mucus on the outside of the bubbles keeps the egg bubbles together until the fry hatch. The fish shown here is a Siamese fighting fish.

## Snail Bubbles

Some violet snails (left) make clusters of mucous bubbles to protect their eggs. Relatives of these snails (below right) use their mucous bubbles as rafts and surf upside down on their bubble rafts on the ocean surface.

## Healthy Mucus

Marine turtles cover their eggs with mucus and sand. The mucus keeps the eggs moist. It may also protect the eggs from bacteria and fungus.

# SALIVA 101

*We may think saliva is gross, but most animals, including humans, couldn't live without it. Saliva helps us taste and swallow food. It also helps our bodies start to break down some foods so we can get energy from them faster. Saliva does some other pretty amazing things, too.*

## Where Does It Come From?

Saliva is made by special cells in glands. Humans have three glands that make saliva on each side of their head. One pair is below our ears, and two pairs are along the backs of our mouths.

## Cool Shapes

Not all salivary glands are the same shape. Many fleas, flies, butterflies, moths, and some other insects use tube-shaped salivary glands to make silk.

## Some Animals Need More!

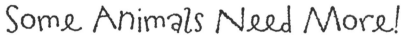

The numbers and shapes of an animals' salivary glands depend on what they eat and how they use saliva. Red pandas and some other grazers have extra-large salivary glands because they need lots of saliva to help them digest plants. Pollen-eating butterflies have extra-large salivary glands, too.

# SALIVA 101

## Fish Tricks

Lampreys are the only fish that have salivary glands. Adult lampreys live on other fish as parasites. To attach onto a fish, a lamprey latches on with circular rows of teeth that work as suckers. Like ticks and mosquitoes, lampreys have chemicals in their saliva that prevent their hosts' blood from clotting.

## Feeding Spit

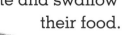

Ants, wasps, and some bees have extra-large salivary glands when they are larvae. These large glands help them make extra saliva. Sometimes they feed their extra saliva to adults!

## Just a Little

Birds that eat wet foods such as fish have small salivary glands.

## No Saliva Here!

Some animals do not have salivary glands. Pelicans may not have salivary glands because their beaks take up so much space in their mouths.

## No Saliva Here, Either

Raccoons do not have salivary glands, either. They often wash their food before eating it, but they are not trying to be super clean. Instead, they use the water like saliva to help them taste and swallow their food.

# WHAT'S IN THERE?

*Saliva is mostly water with some extra — and important — things added in. Besides water, you'll find mucus, salts, minerals, proteins, and other chemicals. Although most animals have saliva, not all saliva is the same.*

## Down the Pike . . .

To get to an animal's stomach, food has to move from the mouth and down a long tube called the esophagus. Saliva helps soften food so it doesn't hurt the esophagus or get stuck. A chewed ball of food mixed with saliva that's ready to swallow is called a bolus.

## Taste Tests

Saliva mixes with food when we chew, making it thinner and wetter. When food is thinner and wetter, it spreads over our taste buds and helps us enjoy more food flavor. Saliva also helps animals taste poisonous foods before swallowing them.

## Cool Drool

Biologists who study moose found a chemical in their saliva that kills fungus in the grass they eat. If their saliva did not kill the fungus, the fungus would kill the moose.

# WHAT'S IN THERE?

## Bye, Bye, Bacteria

Some proteins in saliva attach to bacteria and pull them away from teeth. Other bacteria are swallowed when they stick to the mucus in saliva. Saliva has the same type of antibiotic in it that is found in our tears. Saliva also has minerals that help repair the damage bacteria have done.

When animals lick their wounds or when ants lick their eggs, antibiotics in their saliva help fight infections from bacteria.

## Smile!

Acidic             Neutral             Alkaline

1   2   3   4   5   6   7   8   9   10   11   12   13   14

Saliva also protects teeth in another way. If we eat or drink something that has too much acid in it, our brains quickly tell our bodies to raise the pH of our saliva. Our saliva's pH can change when we just think about lemons or milk! For wild animals that cannot brush their teeth and visit the dentist, saliva is extra important.

## A Fungus Among Us?

Animal mouths might make the perfect habitat for fungi: mouths are dark and damp, just the way fungi like it. Thank goodness saliva has chemicals in it that kill fungi.

## Salty Spit

Some people have more salt in their saliva than others do. This fact explains why the same food can taste very different to different people.

## Say It, Don't Spray It

Sing your favorite song out loud in front of a mirror. Watch how your tongue moves as you form words. Without saliva, you would have a hard time singing or talking!

*Most saliva has special proteins in it called enzymes that help break down food. Not all digestive enzymes are the same because different enzymes break down different types of foods. Most enzyme words end with the -ase suffix.*

## Digest This!

* Octopuses, squid, and cuttlefish use chitin**ase** in their saliva to start breaking down the chitin exoskeletons in their prey.

* Fungus-farming ants use chitin**ase** in their saliva to break down the chitin cell walls in fungi.

* Some bats use lip**ases** in their saliva to get fast energy from the lipids (fats) in their insect prey.

* Some butterflies have a special enzyme in their saliva that breaks down the pollen they eat.

* Scorpions spit on their prey so the enzymes in their saliva will start breaking down their food before they eat it.

* Amyl**ase** in human saliva helps us start digesting sugars in our mouth for fast energy. Many herbivores and omni-vores have amyl**ase** in their saliva, too.

* Many laundry soaps use digestive enzymes to break down food stains.

# WHAT'S IN THERE?

## Changing Times

As people get older, we make less saliva. We also make less saliva when we are nervous or cold, or when we are about to eat something that smells or tastes bad. Having less saliva protects us by making it harder for us to swallow food that may make us sick. When you don't have enough saliva to swallow your food, you gag.

How do people on television shows eat lots of gross things such as insects or worms? They train their minds to believe the gross things are yummy so their salivary glands will keep making saliva.

## Sweet Experiment

Suck on a lollipop for three minutes, getting as much saliva on it as you can. Loosely place the wrapper back on the lollipop. In three hours, unwrap the lollipop. The amylase in your saliva has been hard at work breaking down the lollipop's sugars, making it gooey.

## More? You Want More?

Get three lollipops that are exactly the same. Suck on the first one for three minutes. Place the second one in a bowl of water for three minutes. Leave the third one unwrapped for three minutes. Loosely re-wrap all three lollipops. Check the lollipops in three hours. Why are they different? Why was water a good control for this experiment? Why did you need to control for time?

# LOTS OF SPIT

*People and other animals make more saliva when they are hungry or when they smell food. We even salivate more when we just think about food. We also make extra saliva right before we vomit — doctors think this extra saliva protects our teeth from the stomach acid in vomit.*

## The More, the Merrier

People make between four and eight cups of saliva every day. We make even more saliva when we eat sour or spicy foods.

## Hungry or Sick?

# LOTS OF SPIT

## Drool School

Most babies go through stages when they drool a lot. Young babies who do not yet have strong neck muscles or who keep their mouths open a lot also drool more. You need strong neck muscles and a closed mouth for the swallow reflex to work. Don't believe it? Pretend you're a baby who cannot swallow saliva. How long can you keep your mouth open without drooling?

## Slobber Town

Some dogs slobber more than others. Breeds that have loose mouth skin usually drool a lot. Dogs may also drool more when they are sick and need to see a vet.

## Too Much Info?

Bonobos, a type of primate that lives in Africa, make extra saliva because they swap spit with each other after a fight.

# STICKY SLIME

*Animals that eat a lot of one type of food are called specialists.
These animals often have saliva with extra mucus or extra
water that helps them feed. Sticky saliva has other uses, too.*

## Saliva Seed Balls

Many seed-eating birds use sticky saliva to roll their seeds into balls before eating them.

## Traveling Eggs

Ants cover their eggs with sticky saliva that holds several eggs together, making them easier to carry.

## Dinner Time!

Animals that eat group-living insects such as termites and ants often have lots of sticky saliva. This saliva coats their long, thin tongues, and helps them get lots of insects in every bite. Animals with long tongues and sticky saliva include anteaters, pangolins, armadillos, and green woodpeckers.

# STICKY SLIME

## Savings Account

Gray jays coat small pieces of food with sticky saliva and then "glue" the sticky food in hiding places. When the saliva hardens, it protects the food from bacteria and fungi. During cold winter months, when seeds and insects are harder to find, the jays find and eat their hidden food.

## Spitballs

Some chipmunks use their saliva to help them save food for later. First, they take the shells off their seeds. Next, they roll the seeds into balls that stay together with sticky saliva. The chipmunks do not need to hide their spitballs because other animals do not know they are food.

## Thorn Defense

Giraffes use their sticky saliva to roll their food into a ball before swallowing it. The extra mucus in their sticky saliva helps protect their mouths and esophagus from long thorns on the plants they eat. Sticky saliva comes in handy for nose cleaning, too.

# CLEANING SPIT

Animals need to stay clean for many reasons. Dirty fur, feathers, scales, and skin can make animals sick. The chemicals in saliva that kill bacteria and fungi work like special soaps to protect animals.

## Clean Feet

Jackrabbits lick their feet and use them to clean places their tongues cannot reach.

## Bat Baths

Bats use their tongues for bathing, also. To clean their ears and other places their tongues cannot reach, bats lick their wing thumbs and clean with them.

## Oily Spit

Some insects groom themselves with oily saliva that may help waterproof their exoskeletons.

## Better Than Eye Drops!

Geckos often use the saliva on their tongues to clean their eyes.

# COOLING SPIT

*When saliva evaporates from an animal's fur, it cools it off. Staying cool is very important for most animals, but even more important for animals such as dogs that have small sweat glands.*

## Beat the Heat

When temperatures get too hot, the African spurred tortoise makes extra saliva and spreads it on its forearms. Pretty cool, huh?

## Cool Experiments

When biologists measured how much saliva rats make, they found that the rats made ten times more saliva when the biologists raised the temperature from 75 to 104 degrees F (24 to 40 degrees C). The rats used this extra saliva to give themselves longer and more frequent tongue baths.

## Saliva Spreading

Kangaroos protect themselves from heat by spreading saliva over their front legs. Kangaroos have many branching veins in the areas they cover with spit. Biologists believe saliva spreading helps kangaroos cool down their blood's temperature. Wait, there's more: mother kangaroos spread saliva over their joeys, too.

# TALKING SPIT

*Can you imagine your friends or parents using saliva instead of words to tell you what to do? Does that sound crazy? Or impossible? Well, it's not. Many animals use pheromones in their saliva to share information.*

## You're Cute

Female animals such as fruit flies, boars, and pigs release chemicals in their saliva that tell males they are ready to mate.

Male scorpion flies have extra-large salivary glands and feed saliva to their mates.

## Who Are You?

Soldier termites and worker termites have different pheromones in their saliva.

## X Marks the Spot

How do young mammals know which teat is theirs? By the proteins in their saliva they left there the last time they nursed!

# TALKING SPIT

## Who Needs GPS?

Roaches, termites, and some bees leave saliva on food as a trail that other group members use to find food. Roaches also use alarm chemicals in their saliva to warn other roaches of danger.

*Feed Us!* Honeybee larvae use pheromones in their saliva to tell worker bees to bring them food.

## Hello Again!

Cats, dogs, and many other animals use saliva to recognize their young. When parents clean offspring with tongue baths, proteins from their saliva stay in their young's fur.

# DEFENSE SPIT

*Some animals use their saliva to spread toxins over their bodies to protect themselves. Other animals, such as opossums, use their saliva to send fake messages to predators.*

## Toxic Bubble Spit

What's better for self-defense than five thousand spines? How about a few thousand spines covered in bubbly spit?

Hedgehogs use a behavior called self-anointing. They chew on poisonous toads, plants, or other materials. As they chew, their saliva gets extra bubbly. Then, they use their paws to spread the saliva through their spines.

Zookeepers have also seen hedgehogs covering themselves with bubbly spit when the hedgehogs come across new smells. Biologists have seen young hedgehogs covering themselves with spit when they leave their nests.

## Playing Dead

When opossums feel threatened, they roll on their sides and drool to convince predators they are dead. Sometimes they poop, too. Opossums can play dead for a few minutes or several hours.

# DEFENSE SPIT

## Slow Loris Spit

Slow lorises are endangered primates that live high in trees in Southeast Asia. Biologists believe they may use scents to talk to each other, the way other nocturnal primates do.

When a slow loris feels stress, it rubs a smelly, toxic liquid from a gland near its elbow over its head and neck. Mother lorises cover their young with this liquid when they leave to find food. Young lorises start making their own liquid when they are six weeks old. Sometimes, lorises suck on their elbow liquid, where it mixes with their saliva.

## Why, Why, Why?

Scientists are very curious about the loris's elbow liquid. Do they use it just to warn other lorises about danger and territories? Does it help to keep away fur parasites or predators? If a loris bites another animal when it has elbow toxin in its saliva, does that make the loris the only venomous primate? One thing's for sure: if you're allergic to cats, you should stay away from slow loris saliva because the loris's elbow toxins are similar to the proteins that make some people allergic to cats.

# VENOM SPIT

Reptile venom is a type of super-strong saliva. If you look at the skeletons of many reptiles, you can see spaces in their skulls for large venom glands. These venom glands came from adaptations to salivary glands, the places where saliva is made.

## Science Class

Remember learning about the membranes that hold animal cells together? Some snake venom has an enzyme in it that breaks the cell membranes in their prey. If an animal's red blood cells are broken, it can cause the animal to bleed from the inside. The eyelash viper above lives in Mexico and South and Central America.

## Digesting Venom

Like saliva from other animals, snake saliva has enzymes in it that help digest food. Because snakes eat living prey, their enzymes are very strong, which helps them start digesting the proteins in their prey before it gets to their stomachs. Rattlesnakes have a lot of these muscle-killing enzymes in their saliva venom. When this venom moves into prey, it can stop muscles such as the heart from working.

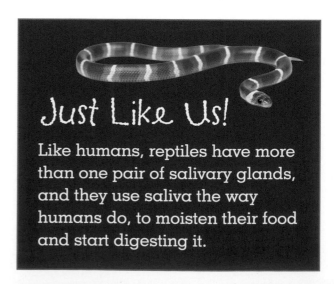

## Just Like Us!

Like humans, reptiles have more than one pair of salivary glands, and they use saliva the way humans do, to moisten their food and start digesting it.

# VENOM SPIT

## Dragon Drool

The strong venom in Komodo dragon saliva lowers their prey's blood pressure, sending them into shock. Why do Komodo dragons need such powerful venom? They feed on very large animals, such as water buffalo, deer, and other dragons.

Mexican beaded lizards (right), bearded dragons, iguanas, and other types of monitor lizards also have venom.

# VENOM SPIT

# VENOM SPIT

## Venom Spit Spray

Spitting cobras do not really spit. Instead, they squeeze the muscles around their venom glands, which sprays venom out through their fangs. Biologists believe spitting cobras use their venom spray to protect themselves from being stepped on by large animals.

Spitting cobras can spray their venom more than six feet and they have very good aim. The venom almost always lands in the victim's eyes, where it can cause blindness for a short time or forever.

There are several types of spitting cobras. They live in Asia and Africa.

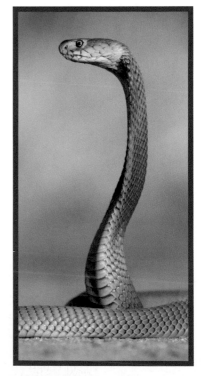

# VENOM SPIT

## Strong Venom, Weak Fangs

Coral snakes have some of the strongest snake venom in the world. Luckily for us, coral snakes have small, weak fangs that cannot break through human skin in a single strike. This coral snake is from the Amazon.

## Mammal Venom?

Some moles, shrews, and shrew-like solenodons use venom in their saliva to stun prey. They do not have fangs, as many venomous snakes do, but make up for it by chewing on prey to deliver extra saliva.

# VENOM SPIT

## Zombie Housecleaning Spit

Female jewel wasps paralyze cockroaches with their stinging venom and then lay their eggs inside them. The venom turns the cockroaches into zombies, which makes them great food and shelter for young wasps. Wasp larvae clean the insides of their roach homes with their saliva, which has bacteria-killing chemicals in it. Sound gross? You might spit-clean the walls of your home, too, if you lived inside a cockroach!

## Spider Bites

More than 30,000 types of spiders live on Earth, and most of them have venom in their saliva. Luckily, humans are not spider prey — spiders only bite people when they feel threatened.

## Saliva on the Fly

Robber flies use venom in their saliva to paralyze flying insects. Their saliva also has digestive enzymes in it that break prey into a soupy mix that robber flies drink.

## Ha, Ha, Made You Drool

The Brazilian wandering spider is one of the most venomous spiders in the world. These spiders can make humans very sick. Their venom also causes people to make extra saliva and mucus.

# UNDERWATER SPIT

*Like land animals, many underwater animals have adaptations in their saliva that help them catch prey and defend themselves.*

## All in the Family

Cuttlefish, squid, and octopuses use digestive enzymes in their saliva to catch prey. These enzymes paralyze their prey, which relaxes their muscles and makes it easier to break into their exoskeletons or shells.

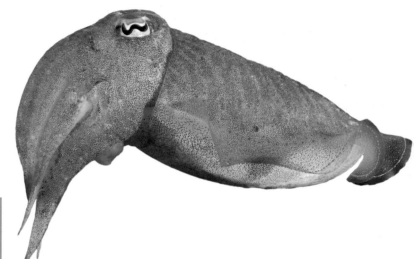

## What? Why? How?

In 1906, two biologists decided to boil octopus saliva for ten minutes. Why would anyone boil octopus saliva? They wanted to know what kind of molecule in the saliva could kill and paralyze crabs, a favorite food of octopuses. After the boiled saliva cooled down, they injected it into crabs and nothing happened. Since protein molecules stop working when they get too hot, this experiment made the biologists believe the octopus toxins were proteins.

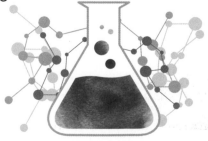

## Sea Snake Spit

Like other members of the cobra family, sea snakes have strong venom that comes from their salivary glands.

# UNDERWATER SPIT

## Deadly Spit

The blue-ringed octopus from Australia, Asia, and Indonesia is well known as one of the most venomous animals in the world. You might think that their venom is just a stronger version of the venom in other octopuses. Actually, the strongest part of the blue-ring venom comes from bacteria living in their salivary glands.

## EGGcellent Spit

Blue-ringed octopuses pass their toxin-making bacteria on to their young. Even developing embryos in their eggs have venom!

# BUILDING SPIT

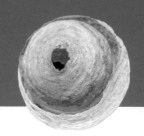

*Is your saliva strong enough to build a castle? Or a nest that could hold a few million termites or a clutch of bird eggs? Nope. Some animals use glue-like mucus in their saliva as a building tool.*

## Saliva Cement

Paper wasps, hornets, and yellow jackets mix their saliva with wood and plant vomit to make their nests. The shape and size of the nest depends on the species and where it lives. These nests are waterproof and very strong.

## Muddy Saliva

Termites build their homes (called mounds) from a mixture of soil, saliva, feces, and vomit. This building mixture is called termite mud.

In some places, termite mounds can be taller than a school bus. In Africa, animals such as yellow mongoose, topi antelope, and cheetahs stand on mounds to look for faraway predators or prey. In Australia, reptiles, birds, and small marsupials use termite mounds as nests.

# BUILDING SPIT

## Swift Spit

Swallows and swifts use sticky saliva to glue twigs together to form their nests. A few types of swifts from Asia make nests from 100 percent saliva! When the saliva dries, the nests are strong enough for swifts to raise their families in them. These swifts have an extra pair of small salivary glands that may help them make extra and/or stickier saliva.

## Soup Time?

People have been eating bird's nest soup made from swift nests for hundreds of years. For a while, biologists were worried that taking so many nests from the wild could cause the swifts to go extinct. Now, some people raise swifts in big buildings and sell the nests as their job. Restaurants buy more than 200 million tons of swift nests every year.

Can you imagine eating bird's nest soup? It's very thick, and chefs usually add some sugar or chicken for extra flavor. Why do so many people eat bird's nest soup if it does not taste good? Some people believe the soup makes them healthier.

# FAMOUS SPITTERS

*Humans spit when something tastes bad or when they are misbehaving. Animals spit for more important reasons: catching prey and escaping predators.*

## Fast Escapes

Need to move fast to escape a predator or catch prey? No worries if you're a water cricket. Just spit on the water around you. The water's surface tension will change, which doubles your travel speed.

## Spitting for Dinner

Walruses spit strong streams of water at the muddy ocean floor. When the mud moves, walruses sometimes find one of their favorite foods, clams.

## Ready, Aim, Fire!

Some types of archerfish hunt for food on land without leaving the water. When they see insects on nearby branches, they shoot a stream of water from their mouths that's strong enough to knock insects into the water, where they quickly become fish food.

# FAMOUS SPITTERS

## Ouch!

One type of assassin bug can spit saliva more than ten times farther than its body's length. These bugs spit painful toxins to defend themselves, not to catch prey. They can also spit five times in one second! How many times can you spit in one second?

## Spit String

Why waste energy chasing prey when you can throw sticky string at it? Spitting spiders hunt this way. The sticky string comes from their salivary glands. They have venom toxins in their saliva, too.

## Stomach Spitters

Camels and llamas mix stomach acid with their saliva and spit the stinky, bubbly mixture at animals and people. The acidic spit smells bad, and works as a warning to back off.

# BITING SPIT

Animals that feed on the blood of other animals often have special chemicals in their saliva that help them get more blood. These chemicals help blood feeders in different ways.

## Let It Flow

Some chemicals in biting saliva make the blood vessels in prey relax. When blood vessels relax, they get wider, which helps blood feeders get more food.

## No Pain, Lots of Gain

Blood suckers such as ticks, flies, and fleas use chemicals in their saliva that stop the animal they are biting from feeling pain. These chemicals also stop swelling, which could slow down blood flow.

## Hide & Seek

Leeches and other biting parasites use chemicals in their saliva that work like a magic hiding cloak. If the biters did not have these chemicals, their host's immune system would know they were there and start working to get rid of them.

# BITING SPIT

## Kind Vampires?

Many people think all bats feed on blood. Really, only a few do. Vampire bats do feed on blood, but they do not suck it. Instead, they make small cuts with their teeth and lap the blood with their tongues, the way house cats lap milk. When vampire bats return to their roosts after a night of blood feeding, they share blood with bats that did not find blood food.

## Ouch!

Have you ever had an insect bite that itches? The swelling and itching come from your immune system responding to the biter's saliva.

## Stylet Straws

To feed on plant juices, stinkbugs insert their sharp stylets into a plant. Next, the stinkbugs protect their stylets by making a case around them with saliva. The case is called a sheath. Stinkbugs may also release watery saliva while eating to dilute the plant's chemical defenses. Aphids can make saliva sheaths around their stylets, too.

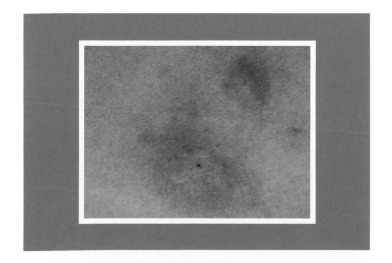

# SICK SPIT

*Many disease-causing organisms live in the salivary glands of animals. Because these glands and the saliva they make are involved in many diseases, doctors are spending a lot of time researching them.*

## Living in Spit

Most people catch malaria when biting mosquitoes move infected blood from one person to another. The parasites that cause malaria live in mosquito saliva in between bites. People with malaria do not have much energy because the parasites get in their blood cells. In Africa, about half a million people die from malaria every year. Above, malaria parasites with blood cells.

## Sleeping Spit

The parasite that causes African sleeping sickness spends part of its life reproducing in the salivary glands of the tsetse (teet zee) fly. When the fly bites a human, the parasites can move from the fly's saliva to the human's blood. African sleeping sickness causes high fevers, rashes, muscle aches, and sometimes death.

## Rabid Drool

Animals catch rabies when saliva from another animal's bite enters their bloodstream. The virus moves through their blood to their brain, where it makes many copies of itself. After that, the virus moves to the infected animal's salivary glands and its saliva. Animals that have rabies drool a lot because their bodies make extra saliva. Rabies can only infect some mammals, including foxes, ferrets, bats, raccoons, skunks, dogs, cats, and humans. Most animals that get rabies will die.

# SICK SPIT

## Sand Fly Spit

Scientists are testing a vaccine made from sand fly saliva that may protect people from skin diseases caused by the fly.

## Bye, Bye, Runny Noses

A new vaccine for dogs and cats may help people with pet allergies. These allergies are often caused by proteins in a pet's saliva when it licks its fur. The vaccine changes the protein. Soon, no more sneezing!

## Monster Spit

A drug made from Gila monster saliva has helped many people with diabetes.

## Vampire Drugs

Scientists are using chemicals from blood-feeding animals to make drugs for humans who have had strokes. The same chemicals that thin blood for feeding ticks, mosquitoes, and vampire bats may help break up blood clots that can cause strokes in people.

# WILD & WACKY

*Some insects use salivary glands to make silk. Sometimes these insects only make silk at certain ages or stages. Not all insect silk comes from salivary glands. Some comes from silk glands on their feet or abdomens.*

## Young Workers

Weaver ant larvae use silk from their salivary glands to hold the leaves together that make their nests. Adults hold the larvae in their mouths and place them where they need silk.

## Saliva Cocoons

Silkworms and some other moths and butterflies spin cocoons from parts of their salivary glands when they are larvae. The cocoons protect them from bad weather and predators as they change into their winged adult bodies.

## Saliva Blankets

Booklice have two salivary glands on each side of their mouths. One pair makes saliva and the other makes silk. They use the silk to make blankets for their colonies to live under.

# WILD & WACKY

## Salty Spit

Saltwater crocodiles have adaptations in their salivary glands that help them absorb extra salt from their bodies.

## Stress Tests

Scientists test the saliva of zoo monkeys for a hormone called cortisol. The amount of cortisol in each monkey's saliva tells them how stressed the animals are.

Scientists can test human saliva for stress hormones, too. In one study, they found that cortisol levels went up after people gave a public speech.

## Electric Spit

Scientists are using saliva to make electricity. So far, it only makes about one microwatt of power, but that's enough to make some types of fuel cells work.

## Drinking Spit

South and Central American Indians make a special corn drink called chicha that uses saliva in the recipe. The amylase in the saliva helps break down starches in the corn.

## Happy Birthday!

Scientists can tell how old someone is by testing their saliva.

# ACKNOWLEDGMENTS

Information from the following individuals, places, and organizations contributed greatly to this book: D.S. Abi Abdallah, Warren Abrahamson, Karina Acevedo-Whitehouse, William C. Agosta, Salim M. Al-Moghrabi, All about Birds/Cornell University, American Chemical Society, American Museum of Natural History, American Society of Ichthyologists and Herpetologists, Eldesouky Ammar, Roland C. Anderson, Bruno B. Andrade, Kimberly D. Ange-van Heugten, Daniele Anina, Aquarium of the Bay, Wolfgang H. Arnold, AskNature, Australian Musuem, Australian Rivers Institute, Dihego de Oliveira Azevedo, Norazlin A. Aziz, Christopher Bailey, Ian T. Baldwin, Aldina Barral, Manoel Barral-Netto, Cowan Belanger, J. Bereiter-Hahn, David Berkowitz, G.J. Binford, A. Pavinski Bitar, Janine Blackwell, Murry Blum, Clemens Bochnig, Jennifer Bombard, Rohan Booker, David T. Booth, David R. Boulware, Ryan Bradley, Thomas Breithaupt, M. Silva Briano, Edmund D. Brodie, Robert Brockie, B.E. Brown, Grant E. Brown, Jonathan Buckley, J.C. Bythell, Roy Caldwell, E.F. Carr, L. Castillo, Caudata Culture, R. F. Chapman, Ronald Chase, Jittipan Chavadej, Celia Churchill, Ben Collins, Robert Condonn, S.M. Correa, A.M. Costa-Leonardo, B. Coughlin, Dave Cowles, Jonathan Cowles, Centers for Disease Control, Scott F. Cummins, Lynn D. Devenport, Mark S. Davies, T.J. Dawson, Bernard M. Degnan, Juan C. DelÁlamo, F. Posadas DelRio, A.J. DeRuiter, Arne Diercks, Clay Dillow, Dimitri Deheyn, Charles D. Derby, Richard DiRocco, Angela E. Douglas, Lee C. Drickamer, S. Dueñas, Stefan H. Eberhard, Rachel Ehrenberg, A.N. Epstein, European Food Information Council, Maresa Fagan, L. A. Farquharson, Sarah Faz, George A. Feldhamer, Gary Felton, Paul L. Fide, Jr., R. Douglas Fields, E. M. Finn, Denis Finnin, F. Fish, Marcel Florkin, Craig E. Franklin, Bryan Fry, Nobuhiro Fusetani, Kristin Gallagher, J.E. Garb, Lisa-Ann Gershwin, Walter M. Goldberg, Jason G. Goldman, Gláucia B. Gonçalves, J.S. González, Barbara Gratzer, DuBose B. Griffin, K.J. Gron, Alexandra S. Grutter, Ramesh C. Gupta, William Hackett, I. Haifig, F.R. Hainsworth, J.R.S. Hales, Celia Hall, David Hall, K. S. Hamilton, Peter J. Hanna, Martin Hardt, Roy Alexander Harrison, Kanehisa Hashimoto, Blair Hedges, Paul Heinrich, R.B. Heredia, Juergen Herler, Gudrun Herzner, Ilo Hiller, Benny Hochner, Anne-Marie Hodge, Jennifer S. Holland, Henk-Jan Hoving, Don Hunsaker, István Imre, Y. Itagaki, Mary Ann Jabra-Rizk, Jarred R. Jenkins, K. Johannesson, Nicholas S. Johnson, D. Jones, C. Barker Jørgensen, Kaieteur National Park, S. Kamhawi, Melissa Kaplan, Isabella Kappner, Julia Kästner, Philipp Al Khatib, KidsHealth.org, Megan Kierzek, K.C. Kim, S. M. Kisia, Thomas Kleinteich, Kritaya Kongsuwan, S. Krane, Carey Krajewski, Harold W. Krenn, Chitraporn Kuanpradit, Samantha Lafontaine, Janice Lai, Sam Lai, Juan Lashera, Wing-Kee Lee, Guy Levy, Map of Life, E.R. Lillehoj, Bruce E. Logan, S. López, MarineBio Conservation Society, Marine Education Society of Australasia, Gustavo Ferreira Martins, H. Marquis, Solange Marques-Silva, Jennifer A. Mather, A.G. Matoltsy, Maui Ocean Center, Neil McDaniel, Rod McDonald, Donald M. McKinstry, Stefan Meldau, S. Mendez, Adriana De Lima Mendonça, C. Meneses, Joseph F. Merritt, Metropolitan Oceanic Institute & Aquarium, W.L. Meyer, Eva Millesi, Monterey Bay Aquarium and Research Institute, Mariella Moon, C.E. Mueller, Dietland Müller-Schwarze, Thomas M. Murphy, Murray-Darling Basin Authority, Darren Naish, K. Nakanishi, Ruth R. Do Nascimento, Ella A. Naumova, A.D. Needham, Hans L. Nemeschkal, T.P. Ng, Phil Nixon, F. Oliveira, Opossum Society of the United States, Oregon Health and Science University, Prancing Papio, Stephanie Pappas, J.J. Park, C. John Parmenter, Roger Pearson, Penn State College of Agricultural Sciences, Brian M. Peters, Andrea D. Phillott, K.A. Pitt, Christopher Putnam, M.J. Ranilla, K.S. Richards, Claudio Richter, Bruce Robison, Javier Rodriguez, M.G. Rodríguez, Lynn L. Rogers, B.K. Rubin, Jennifer G. Rumney, A.Z.M. Salem, S.H. Saltin, Tudor Sandulescu, Mark A. Scheper, Stefan Schuster, ScienceLine, José Eduardo Serrão, Syed Waliullah Shah, Sara El Shaye, Stephen J. Simpson, Tane Sinclair-Taylor, Carlos E. Silva, Katherine A. Sloman, Andrew M. Smith, Smithsonian National Zoological Park, Prasert Sobhon, Society for Science & the Public, Marcos Franklin Sossal, South Carolina Department of Natural Resources, Prapee Sretarugsa, R. Stafford, Kathrin Steckbauer, C. Swann, Jessie Szalay, Clarissa R. Teixeira, Ross Tellam, Martin Thiel, Craig Thorburn, Aleš Tomčala, John Tooker, A.S. Tucker, United States Department of Agriculture, University of California-Santa Barbara ScienceLine, Adalberto Luis Val, J.G. Valenzuela, Aart J. E. VanBel, Lucie Vaníčková, J.J. Ventura, Stephen H. Vessey, Nicolas Vidal, Dietrich VonKnorre, J.A. Voynow, Peter Waldie, Manfred Walzl, P.J. Weldon, S.W. Werneke, Mark Willcox, Torsten Will, G.A. Williams, David Wong, James B. Wood, Jennifer L. Wortham-Neal, Banglao Xu, Kazuo Yamazak, Ed Yong, José Cola Zanuncio, José Salazar Zanuncio, Jr., Dongni Zhang, Zhenjun Zhao, Jingsong Zhu, Marc Zimmer, Stefan Zimmer, and P.A. Zobel-Thropp.

# ACKNOWLEDGMENTS

Gratitude is extended to the following photographers and photographic sources for their creative contributions.

**From Shutterstock:** 2NatS, Abbydog, Akiyoko, Alan Poulson Photography, Alexsvirid, Solodov Alexey, Andreas Altenburger, Andaman, AndChisPhoto, B. Toy Anucha, Ronald van der Beek, O. Bellini, Bildagentur Zoonar GmbH, BlackeagleEMJ, Blamb, Bluehand, Jeremy Brown, Vittorio Bruno, Aleksandr Bryliaev, Andrew Burgess, Jose Luis Calvo, Chelsea Cameron, Rich Carey, Chesky, ChinKC, Nantawat Chotsuwan, Lars Christensen, R. Classen, Antonio Clemens, Andre Coetzer, Creations, Csabacz, Cynoclub, Ethan Daniels, Darios, Davemhuntphotography, Decade3d/Anatomy Online, De-2marco, Pan Demin, Designua, Di Studio, Digitalbalance, Robert Eastman, Frolova Elena, Biro Emoke, Dirk Ercken, ERIC I, Erni, Tiplyashina Evgeniya, David Evison, Iakov Filimonov, Steven Fish, Fivespots, Mike Flippo, Fotos593, Four Oaks, Nick Fox, Foxterrier2005, J. Gade, Volodymyr Goinyk, R. Gombarik, Graphic Compressor, HeinzTeh, H. Helene, Vitalii Hulai, Ifong, Indigolotos, Irin-k, IrinaK, Tischenko Irina, Eric Isselee, Wichitpong Katwit, Cathy Keifer, Larry B. King, Levent Konuk, Vadim Kozlovsky, Irina Kozorog, Volodymyr Krasyuk, Tamara Kulikova, Kurt_G, Lori Labrecque, Seth LaGrange, George Lamson, Henrik Larsson, LauraD, Valeriy Lebedev, Kit Leong, Lik Studio, Littlesam, J.Y. Loke, Michael Lynch, C.K. Ma, Cosmin Manci, Joe McDonald, Brandy McKnight, Vladimir Kogan Michael, Mikecphoto, Jon Milnes, Mnoor, Andre Mueller, Christian Musat, Jonathan Nackstrand, Nattanan726, Neryx.com, Stacey Newman, Byelikova Oksana, OneSmallSquare, Oolulu, Jakkrit Orrasri, Bernatskaya Oxana, Pakhnyushchy, Adam Paradi, Passenier, PathDoc, Somyot Pattana, Andrey Pavlov, Perutskyi Petro, Photokin, Picturepartners, Daniel Poloha, Stuart G. Porter, Prajit48, Mitch R., Yusran Abdul Rahman, Alexander Raths, Morley Read, Reptiles4all, RioPatuca, Roblan, Ivaschenko Roman, Paul Rommer, Jason Patrick Ross, R. Gino Santa-Maria, Susan Schmitz, Sciencepics, Serg_dibrova, Serg64, Khamidulin Sergey, Sergey Skleznev, Andrew Skolnick, cott T. Slattery, Carolina K. Smith, Danny Smythe, Beverly Speed, Stasis Photo, Aleksey Stemmer, David P. Stephens, Stockpix4u, Allen McDavid Stoddard, Kuttelvaserova Stuchelova, Studio 37, Suz7, Sydeen, TechWizard, Shunfa Teh, Decha Thapanya, TinnaPong, Anatoly Tiplyashin, Ugreen 3S, Marco Uliana, Kristina Vackova, VaLiza, Marek Velechovsky, Aleksei Verhovski, Vlad61, Kirsanov Valeriy Vladimirovich, Vaclav Volrab, Wiratchai Wansamngam, Tony Wear, WilleeCole Photography, Michiel de Wit, Wonderisland, Worldswildlifewonders, Xpixel, Pan Xunbin, Davydenko Yuliia, Sonsedska Yuliia, and Jiang Zhongyan

**From Other Sources:** CDC, CDC/Mae Melvin, Discover Waitomo, Russ Hopcroft/Institute of Marine Science/University of Alaska-Fairbanks/(UAF)/NOAA, Joana Garrido, James Lindsey/Ecology of Commanster (Licensed under CC BY-SA 3.0 via Commons/Wickipedia), Murray-Darling Basin Authority, NOAA/CBNMS, NOAA Okeanos Explorer Program, Ben Reichardt/Getty Images, Denis Riek, Gunther Schmida, Ron Shimek, Linda Snook, and Norbert Wu/Getty Images.

**Appreciation is also extended to the following students and staff at Hall Fletcher Elementary School in Asheville, North Carolina for beta testing feedback:** Ms. Beverly McBrayer (Library Media Program Director); Alana, Amara, Ana'ya, Charlie, Elijah, Gabby, Gavin, James, Jasper, Josiah, Julian, Leona, Kayjon, Kyleah, Magnolia, Naomi, Phoebe, Stella, and Yasaret from Mr. Tomas Seijo's fourth grade class; and Adreyona, Alexander, Ayana, Brenda, Brooklyn, Cheyenne, Danielle, DaRoyal, Elle, Jeremiah, Keedrick, Leah, Manuel, Marquavious, Rayne, Tamylah, and Xev in Ms. Rebe Shaw-Cooke's fourth grade class.

## Wonder Why . . .

Why are these wolves greeting each other with their tongues out? Like many other mammals, wolves use scents that come from pheromones in their saliva to get information about other wolves. Young wolves also lick the muzzles of adults in their pack so the adults will regurgitate (puke) food into their mouths.

# INDEX & GLOSSARY

**BACTERIA:** Single-celled organisms that do not have organelles

**CARBOHYDRATE** (also called sugar): A type of organic molecule made from carbon, oxygen, and hydrogen. Simple carbohydrates give animals energy; complex carbohydrates make structures such as cell walls in plants and exoskeletons in arthropods.

**ECOSYSTEM:** The living and nonliving parts of an environment that function together as a group

**ENZYME:** A type of protein that speeds up reactions

**GLAND:** An organ that secretes materials such as mucus or hormones

**HABITAT:** The home for an organism or a group of organisms

**LIPID** (also called fat): A type of organic molecule made from carbon, oxygen, and hydrogen that provides long-term energy to animals

**PROTEIN:** A large molecule made from amino acids; some proteins are enzymes

**TOXIN:** A compound that can cause illness or damage

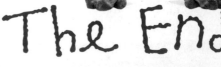

The End!